AF264874

NOT JUST A TEACHER

NOT JUST A TEACHER

A Poetic Tribute to Teachers

TARANGA KENT

TK Publishing

Copyright © 2022 by Taranga Kent

All rights reserved.

Taranga Kent asserts her moral right to be identified as the author of this book.

No part of this book may be reproduced in any manner whatsoever without written permission except in the case of brief quotations embodied in critical articles and reviews.

A catalogue record for this book is available from the National Library of New Zealand.

ISBN: 978-0-473-62481-1 soft cover

First Printing, 2022
Printed in Australia

Taranga Kent
tarangak@gmail.com

To all you dedicated educators out there
who go above and beyond
for the kids in your care,
because you care.

ACKNOWLEDGEMENT

Thank you to R.de Wolf – author, friend, cheerleader and chief pants-kicker, for giving me the support and encouragement I needed to write my words. This book would never have become a reality without you. I can't thank you enough xox

Not Just A Teacher

So often we are defined by what we do for a living
Well, I'm a teacher
But I'm also a gardener
I plant seeds
I tend to your needs
I propagate
I nurture and nourish
Providing optimal conditions for growth
In an organic environment
Imparting sunshine and warmth
On the most dismal of days
Your blossoming and flourishing
Is my greatest reward

I'm a teacher
But I'm also an electrician
A lot of energy is involved
My task is to shed light
And brighten your day
I empower you
Acting as a circuit breaker
Disrupting long-established cycles
I deal with bright sparks
And live wires
I keep you grounded
I make connections
Untangling crossed wires
So currents can flow
I'm not easily shocked
I cherish those 'lightbulb moments'
They give me the reason and faith to carry on

I'm a teacher
But I'm also a plumber
You never know what's in the pipeline
I deal with a lot of crap
And endure extremely bad smells
I can predict when the waterworks are about to start
And stem their flow
It can be draining
But somebody's got to do it

I'm a teacher
But I'm also a glazier
I install windows
Through which to view
Pathways and possibilities
I know your 'pane'
I witness it every day
I do my best to repair
The shattered parts of you
I can see through you
I know that tough exterior
You display to the world
Is just a shield
For your heart
To deflect your hurt

I'm a teacher
But I'm also an auto mechanic
I have a wide range of tools in my toolbox
I look under the hood for clues
And try to find the key to what drives you
Conducting diagnostic tests
Adjusting the steering
So you don't get pulled to the wrong side
Oiling the cogs to keep them turning
Making sure you've got gas in the tank
Dealing with overheated engines
Blown gaskets
And cracked heads
Tune-ups occur regularly
Now and then
I might grind your gears
But it's always with the best of intentions

I'm a teacher
But I'm also a doctor
I have a lot of patience
I deal with blood, snot and tears
Coughs and sneezes in my face
And occasionally tragic events
I make assessments
Based on thorough examinations
I conduct tests and advise you of the results
I analyse my findings and make a diagnosis
Devising a course of action
Which you won't adversely react to
I evaluate outcomes and make adjustments
I prescribe things to do at home
To increase your chances of improving
I track your progress
I refer you to specialists where appropriate
I'm a professional

I'm a teacher
But I'm also a nurse
No two days are ever the same
I do what I can to heal the hurt
That's on the inside as well as the outside
Grazed knees, stubbed toes
Broken arms from falling off monkey bars
Drive-you-crazy itching from eczema and flea bites
Breathless asthmatics at athletics
Nits falling onto books from bowed heads
These are the simple things to deal with
Patching up the open wounds left by bullying
Easing the pain of name-calling for being different
When all you want to do is fit in
Dealing with internal bruises from
"I'm not going to be your friend"
Repairing damage
Done by abusive or neglectful parents
These are just some of the tougher challenges
Active listening, hugs and compassion
Are my magic medicine

I'm a teacher
But I'm also a proctologist
Groping around in the dark
Difficult to see
The light at the end of the tunnel
Sometimes the middle finger
Is aimed at me

I'm a teacher
But I'm also a builder
I follow plans
I aim to hit the nail on the head
And hammer things into you
I am a cornerstone
I lay a strong foundation
A solid base
From which to rise up and face the world
I construct a sound framework
So you can unlock doors to new and exciting spaces
I add shape and form to raw materials
I provide structure and consistency
I offer shelter from the storm that is life

I'm a teacher
But I'm also a miner
I dig deep to discover what's hidden underneath
I never know what I'm going to find
Lurking beneath the surface
I chip away
To reveal what's behind years of built up walls
I polish diamonds in the rough
And find real gems
It can be hard to see where I'm going
But I know my destination

I'm a teacher
But I'm also a secretary
I take detailed notes about significant events
I submit incident reports
To document every little scrape and scrap
I write newsletters
To keep families in touch
With what's happening in your world
I make appointments
For parents to come and air their concerns
I send and receive correspondence
About the absence of uniforms ...
And swimming gear ... and stationery ...and hats ...
I get messages
About absences from school
The presence of nits and asthma
Bad moods and attitudes
I organise travel
To camps and excursions to broaden horizons
I make phone calls
To chase up permission slips
So you don't miss out on class trips
It's not just working 9 to 5, Dolly!

I'm a teacher
But I'm also a health and safety officer
I'm trained in first aid
I minimise your exposure to dangerous situations
I patrol the playground to ensure you don't get hurt
I identify perils within the environment
I write risk assessments
For education outside the classroom
I advise you not to share food and drinks and saliva
I regularly sterilise things
That end up in little mouths
i.e. everything
I discourage you from chewing on lead pencils ...
And toes ... and snot ... and other kids ... and ....

I'm a teacher
But I'm also a mediator
Conflict resolution is a regular occurrence
I intervene in situations before they get out of hand
And also when they are already out of control
I step in between children who are bigger than me,
Risking my own physical safety to protect yours
Compromise and negotiation are taught skills
I am a voice of reason
I defuse tension
And create a pathway out of the corner
You backed yourself into

I'm a teacher
But I'm also an actor
I usually perform solo
However I am just one of a cast of many
I prefer a live audience
Body language, facial expressions and gestures
Help to get my message across
I do my own stunts
I am subject to reviews and critique
By people who have no idea
How hard this occupation is
I turn on a smile
Even on my darkest days
I play my part and expect you to play yours
There's no shortage of drama!

I'm a teacher
But I'm also an author
I specialise in character development
I create stimulating settings
I find solutions to problems
I've been known to get tense
And occasionally I lose the plot!
I lead you through this current chapter
Toward what I hope will be a happy ending

I'm a teacher
But I'm also an editor
I scrutinise your writing
Providing guidance
To proofread and polish
Rework and refine
Strengthen and structure
Honing the skills
To bring forth your voice
And tell your own stories

I'm a teacher
But I'm also a security guard
A clean criminal record is mandatory
Crowd control is part of my job description
I patrol the playground to ensure your safety
I permit only authorised people to pick you up
In the event of a lockdown
I take you to the safest place to wait it out
I shield you from harm
Potentially putting my own life on the line to do so

I'm a teacher
But I'm also a project manager
I lead from the front
I generate realistic and achievable schedules
Ensure attainment within stipulated time frames
Create concepts
And implement transformational plans
From inception to completion
I devise strategies to deal with risks and issues
Preparing for every eventuality
I build strong links with stakeholders
I utilise negotiation skills
I monitor progress and milestones
I'm constantly working under pressure
I think on my feet
I deliver change

I'm a teacher
But I'm also an event planner and fundraiser
Spending days out of my weekend
And time away from my own kids
At galas and garage sales
Car washes and quiz nights
Contributing to bake sales
Organising raffles and rewards
Selling tickets to family and friends
Collecting money from sales
Movie nights and mufti days
'...-a-thon' events and art auctions
Discos and day trips
Camps and coin trails
Talent quests and school productions
(Where I'm called upon to be a sound engineer,
lighting technician, stagehand, director, producer,
makeup artist, set designer, prop maker, musician,
script writer, costume maker ... You name it)

I'm a teacher
But I'm also a fortune teller
I do readings
I never know what's going to be on the cards
From one day to the next
I foresee what the future might hold for you
I wish I had a crystal ball

I'm a teacher
But I'm also a politician
I aim to make a difference
I'm a seasoned campaigner
Making considered decisions
Advocating for those without a voice
Or a platform to be heard
I attend copious meetings
Building relationships is paramount
I get to hold a lot of babies!

I'm a teacher
But I'm also a librarian
I shelve my own problems when I walk in the door
I'm passionate about the value of reading
I reinforce that you can't judge a book by its cover
I'm used to things being overdue
I carefully select texts to stimulate your mind
I teach you to research
So you can find out for yourself
I enable you to explore
Other times, other places, other lives
I empower you
To imagine, to question, to dream

I'm a teacher
But I'm also a hairdresser
Breaking things down into strands
Keeping an eye out for nits
Demonstrating scissor skills
I'm expected to stay up to date
With the latest trends
I cater for individual styles
Adding highlights to catch attention
I offer a listening ear

I'm a teacher
But I'm also a counsellor
You tell me what's going on at home
Everything from sibling rivalry
To disclosure of abuse
I offer support, guidance,
Coping tools and strategies
I let you know that you are important
And that you have been heard

I'm a teacher
But I'm also an engineer
I build bridges
And connect communities
I design smooth pathways
I establish stable infrastructure
That I hope will last a lifetime

I'm a teacher
But I'm also an interior designer
I maximise the available space
Taking personalities into account
I choose materials carefully to suit your style
Furnishing rooms to create
A comfortable, inclusive environment
Conducive to fulfilling your needs
I spend time during weekends and holidays
Decorating walls
I curate and display your work for all to see
So you can be proud of your achievements
I add brightness to the world you enter daily
To lift your spirits
And bring warmth to your surroundings

I'm a teacher
But I'm also a detective
I figure things out as I go
Looking for clues
Recording evidence
Investigating allegations
Determining where to next
Asking relevant probing questions
Deciding what's true or false
Getting to the bottom of the matter
A finder of lost socks and jumpers,
Pencils and toys
Solving the mysteries of the universe

I'm a teacher
But I'm also an inventor
I look for creative solutions
To diverse issues
I am an innovator
Constantly refining my practice
In order to improve outcomes
I reinvent myself every year
For each new cohort
I cultivate curiosity
I reflect on how things can be made better

I'm a teacher
But I'm also a contortionist
Flexibility and stamina are crucial
I need to have eyes in the back of my head
I occasionally get bent out of shape
But I'll bend over backwards for you

I'm a teacher
But I'm also a statistician
I collect and collate data
Analyse it
And generate reports
Identifying trends and gaps
Probability, predictions and percentages
Are all part of the equation
I take a wide range of factors into account
I attempt to be as accurate as possible
But there's always a margin for error

I'm a teacher
But I'm also a magician
I can make tears disappear
I transform mundane things
Into interesting experiences
I create my own resources out of thin air
I make magic happen on a daily basis!

I'm a teacher
But I'm also a photographer
I capture moments in time
I take snapshots which reflect the big picture
Focus
Composition
And development
All play a part
I turn negatives into positives in a flash
I'm often in the dark

I'm a teacher
But I'm also a sculptor
I start with a general outline
Refining it along the way
Carefully considering
Form and function
Whittling away the rough edges
Shaping you for what lies ahead
Helping to create the future you

I'm a teacher
But I'm also a coach
I plan, organise and conduct practice sessions
Training, motivating and advising
I champion your cause
Success depends upon your active participation
I assist you to set achievable goals
I monitor your performance and analyse the stats
To identify where improvements can be made
I adjust techniques
Taking into account your strengths and challenges
I have high expectations
I push you to go beyond your limits
To persevere
To do more than you think you can
I give you strategies to play the long game
After all, it's a marathon not a sprint

I'm a teacher
But I'm also a firefighter
Springing into action at the sound of a bell
I'm constantly putting out fires
And responding to false alarms
There's a tendency to overheat
Access to water is important
(And so is having a strong bladder)
I often see red!

I'm a teacher
But I'm also an entertainer
I perform in front of a crowd
Encouraging audience participation
I keep you engaged for hours on end
I've been known to sing, dance and tell jokes
(Usually very badly on all three counts)
I cheer you up when you're having a bad day
I'm a juggler
With multiple balls in the air at one time
It can be a real balancing act

I'm a teacher
But I'm also a tour guide
I plan where to go and how to get there
I take you to places you never knew existed
I accompany you in exploring new horizons
You may come with baggage
That I can help to unpack
I ensure you have a passport
To a better future
We go on this journey together

I'm a teacher
But I'm also a navigator
I look for signs to show me the way
I advise the best path to follow
To arrive in the shortest possible time
I help you set a sustainable pace
I provide instruction and direction
I'll do my best to get you there
But the rest is up to you

I'm a teacher
But I'm also a pilot
It's necessary to be aware
Of what's happening around me
My main aim is to elevate you
Not going too high or too low
Once I get you on board
I can transport you from one place to another
Establishing an optimum trajectory
To get you where you need to go
My moral compass assisting navigation
There are times when you don't turn up
And I carry on without you
Safety is a top priority
It's a huge responsibility
Your life is in my hands
I sometimes feel as if
I'm building the plane as I'm flying it

I'm a teacher
But I'm also a superhero
I stand on the shoulders of giants
I espouse the merits of good over evil
I don't possess a silver bullet
My weapons are more subtle
But I carry the power to change lives
I will move mountains for you
I give you hope for a better future

I'm a teacher
But I'm also a locksmith
I open doors
Gaining access
To where you want to go
I supply keys
To unlock
New worlds and opportunities

I'm a teacher
But I'm also a substitute parent
A responsibility I take very seriously
I'm entrusted with your care
I spend as much time with you as your family does
In some cases more
I offer a support network
A confidante to share your thoughts and feelings
I teach good manners
How to tie shoelaces
How to blow your nose
How to care for your belongings
And other people
I teach you how to walk before you run
I wish I had a dollar
For every time I've been called "Mum"

I'm a teacher
But I'm also a storyteller
You like hearing about my childhood
What school was like 'in the old days'
The games kids liked to play back then
And the toys we played with
But especially about how we were disciplined
I tell you anecdotes about my life outside of school
Yet you are still surprised and excited
When you see me at the supermarket
You seem to think I live in the classroom
Not unreasonable
Considering the amount of time I spend there

I'm a teacher
But I'm also an accountant
There's a mountain of paperwork
It can be a numbers game
Mathematical competency is required
There are assets, liabilities and deficits
I know all about tight budgets
I collate information and prepare detailed reports
I identify data anomalies and underlying issues
And perform reconciliations
I'm always attempting to achieve balance
Occasionally I deal with liquidity issues
This career can be very taxing

I'm a teacher
But I'm also an architect
I formulate a vision
My plans are tailored to meet individual needs
I liaise with you at every step of the way
Gathering information to assist me
I look at all the dimensions
Including detailed elevations
I decide what materials to use
And how best to use them
Remedial works can be necessary

I'm a teacher
But I'm also a chef
I feed your mind
Modifying ingredients to see what works best
Approaching each day in bite size pieces
I work in a pressure cooker environment
Being organised is essential
I am passionate about what I do
There's a method to my madness
Some of you I have beef with
Some of you drive me bananas
Some of you are as sweet as pi
The takeaways are life-long learning skills
Your delight in your own achievements
Is the cherry on top
There's not mushroom for anything else in my life
By the time I get home I feel like a vegetable
Some days are just nuts
Lucky I'm not allergic
Because teaching is my jam!

I'm a teacher
But I'm also a preacher
I offer guidance and pastoral care
I deliver sermons
About a selection of Deadly Sins
Most commonly sloth and wrath
I paraphrase some of the 10 Commandments
Thou shalt not steal
Becomes
"Don't take what doesn't belong to you"
Thou shalt not bear false witness against your
neighbour
Equates to
"No it **wasn't** him, I just saw you do it!"
I frequently pray for miracles!

I'm a teacher
But I'm also a cleaner
Of projectile spews
And random as poos
Food on floors
Paint on doors
Beans in ears
Ketchup tears
Gum in hair
Or stuck to chairs
Broken glass
In science class
Marker on walls
Bean bag balls
Abandoned stinky solo socks
Odd stuff in the dress up box

I'm a teacher
But I'm also an animal trainer
I teach you how to sit and stay
And poop in the right place
I discourage you from biting
And reward you with praise or treats
When you make the right choices

I'm a teacher
But I'm also a ship's captain
I ensure that everyone is on board
I steer you in the right direction
Maintaining a steady course
Riding the waves with you
Keeping you afloat
We weather the storms together
There are times I am stern
But I don't expect you to bow!

I'm a teacher
But I'm also a judge
I listen to arguments from both sides
I consider the long term consequences
I make objective decisions
Based on all the evidence
I hand out sentences
That end with a period
Which makes you stop
And take a breath

I'm a teacher
But I'm also a scaffolder
Providing support and stability
At a range of different levels
Making sure connections are secure
Advancing in successive stages
With the goal
Of attaining great heights

I'm a teacher
But I'm also a supermodel
I am required to be well groomed
And keep to a dress code
I show samples and examples
I follow what's in fashion
I prefer to be natural
But at times I make up as I go along
There are quick changes
I demonstrate quiet confidence
And an even demeanour
I adopt different styles
I bring all the elements together
To attain the desired outcome
I put one foot in front of the other
To make it through the day
I take it all in my stride
Holding my head high
And walking the talk
I have attitude

I'm a teacher
But I'm also a service technician
Figuring out the photocopier's latest issue
Tempted to deliver a swift kick
For a quick fix
The paper always seems to run out
When I'm using it
Bob Marley's 'Jammin' is a regular refrain

I'm a teacher
But I'm also a welder
Making connections
Melding minds and materials
It may be a grind at times
But can also be riveting

I'm a teacher
But I'm also a shepherd
For obvious reasons -
It can be like herding sheep!
I tend to my flock
Oversee your growth and development
Then move you on to another pasture

I'm a teacher
But I'm also a social worker
I'm responsible for dealing with
Some at risk little humans
And their families
Identifying patterns and contributing factors
That influence how you learn and behave
Aiming to improve outcomes
Providing psychological first aid
Teaching you coping mechanisms
You can draw on throughout your life
Handling sensitive information
Upholding confidentiality
I endeavour to be a good role model
As these might be few and far between
Relationships are integral
I guide and support you
Towards a positive future
I walk alongside you
I'm there to pick you up if you fall

I'm a teacher
But I'm also a barista
Coffee keeps me going
Enough said!

I'm a teacher
But I'm also an orchestral conductor
I deal with a diverse range of instruments
Including wind
It's a challenge to get everyone playing in unison
Lots of arm waving and gesticulations are involved
A great deal of tuning up is required

I'm a teacher
But I'm also a bricklayer
Cementing materials together
Adding one brick at a time
Making sure each layer is secure
Before adding another
It may be slow and painstaking
But the result makes it all worthwhile

I'm a teacher
But I'm also a mountaineer
Preparation is vital
It's about putting one foot in front of the other
Focusing on a single step at a time
Avoiding making mountains out of molehills
Each day presenting an Everest to knock off
Enjoying the sweet success of summiting

I'm a teacher
But I'm also a pirate
Sailing off into uncharted territory
Each and every year
In search of great gains
I impart pearls of wisdom
Encouraging you to go for gold
I find diamonds and jewels
Unseen from the surface
It takes persistence
And a lot of digging
But it's worth it
When you discover treasure

About the Author

Teaching is the last thing Taranga Kent ever thought she would do when she left school to work in an office. A chance meeting with a teacher trainee at her child's school Christmas party years later inspired her to give it a go. She now has over two decades of teaching behind her. Taranga began to write for pure enjoyment, with thoughts most often coming to her as she lay in bed waiting for sleep to come. These late-night efforts would end up on scraps of paper in a drawer with no intention of them ever being seen by anyone else. Joining a local writers' group and receiving positive feedback on her work from others led her to consider getting published as a realistic possibility. Not Just A Teacher is the long-awaited result.

www.ingramcontent.com/pod-product-compliance
Lightning Source LLC
Chambersburg PA
CBHW061048050726
47592CB00004B/1626